TRANSFORMING
ALTERNATIVE EDUCATION

*"From Alternative Education
Student to Administrator"*

DR. LATESHIA
WOODLEY
LPC, NCC

authorHOUSE®

AuthorHouse™
1663 Liberty Drive
Bloomington, IN 47403
www.authorhouse.com
Phone: 1 (800) 839-8640

Published by AuthorHouse   06/16/2016

ISBN: 978-1-5049-7740-1 (sc)
ISBN: 978-1-5049-7741-8 (hc)
ISBN: 978-1-5049-8060-9 (e)

Print information available on the last page.

Any people depicted in stock imagery provided by Thinkstock are models, and such images are being used for illustrative purposes only. Certain stock imagery © Thinkstock.

This book is printed on acid-free paper.

CONTENTS

ACKNOWLEDGEMENTS

I am humbly grateful to God for the opportunity to share this most important work. This would not be possible without the guidance and support from many administrators, teachers, and student support personnel who paved the way for this project. I thank my family for their support and encouragement. I also acknowledge and humbly thank my partners, students, friends and supporters of Dynamic Achievement Solutions, LLC.

DEDICATION

This book is dedicated to all the principals, teachers and student support personnel who work with at risk students. Thank you for your willingness to go the extra mile, to find a way out of no way and for your tenacity to make what seems sometimes to be impossible possible. Thank you for making a difference in the lives of these at-promise students; looking past what they present in their present and unselfishly investing in their future.

PREFACE

The French proverb which states "The More Things Change The More They, Stay The Same" sets the stage for this book, *Transforming Alternative Education*. Although the concept of alternative education was established in the 1970's, today many alternative education programs have not transformed to meet the needs of their students.

This project was birthed out of a desire to bring awareness to the need to transform alternative education as a means to reduce the revolving door of high school drop outs entering and exiting our programs.

This book is about viewing alternative education through the lens of being an alternative education student and then becoming a turnaround leader working with schools to transform alternative education programs. This book celebrates the successful work of many alternative schools making a difference in the lives of students and highlights the areas in which additional work is needed.

Thank you for the opportunity to share both my personal journey of being an alternative school student and my professional journey as a turnaround leader of an urban alternative school with you.

Forever Grateful,

Dr. Teshia

INTRODUCTION

Seldom, in life we are given what I consider a once in a lifetime opportunity; an opportunity that mean so to you that you can't place a monetary value on it. I was afforded such an opportunity. Exactly twenty years after graduating from my alternative high school, I was offered a position as a turnaround leader to come back and lead a school improvement transformation initiative at that very same institution. Although I had spent several years prior working with transformation initiatives in alternative education settings, nothing could prepare me for the overwhelming flood of emotions that accompanied me on the way to school and home each day. I could not block the scenes of memories from the past that infiltrated my mind like infomercials establishing a case for the need for transformation.

It was amazing to see that not much had changed at the school in twenty years. New faces were there, but the same issues and mindsets were pervasive. The issues with leadership, low expectations of students, dysfunctional team dynamics, adult centered versus student centered policies and procedures, and a lack of resources and family and community support were ever present at my alternative school like many alternative schools across the country. This book serves as call to action for those who want to reform alternative education. Once we know better, we must do better. This book will share some of the tools used in the successful transformation initiatives that I was afforded the opportunity to implement, in hopes that it will provide a catalyst as well as a framework to guide your work with at promise youth.

MY STORY: AN ALTERNATIVE EDUCATION STUDENT

My story began in a very small town named Eufaula, Alabama. I had many strikes against me from the very beginning: where I grew up, the family I was born to, my race and my sex. According to an article written in the New York Times by Harvard Economist Nathaniel Henderson, a child born into poverty living in Eufaula has a 2.7 percent chance of achieving success. So my journey from struggling student to educational leader is perhaps an outlier. My mother was a teen mother who gave birth to me at fourteen years of age. She continued a generational cycle of teenaged motherhood that existed in my family dating all the way back to the time of slavery. My grandmother was the mother of seven children. My grandmother and grandfather divorced when I was a baby, so needless to say I was raised by single parent house hold. We lived in a public housing project in a three-bedroom apartment. The four girls slept in one room; the three boys slept in the other. I slept in the bed with my grandmother until I was in middle school and most of my aunts and uncles had moved out.

Both my maternal and my paternal grandmothers and grandfathers never graduated from high school. My father's mother could not read or write. Only four out of my grandmother's seven children graduated from high school. None of my aunts or uncles from either my mother's or father's side of the family graduated from college with a four year degree. My mother's mother did not know how to drive, nor did she ever own a car. She worked as a housekeeper and cook.

Both my parents were both physically and emotionally unavailable. My father was the town drunk and drug addict, and my mother was a workaholic who moved to Atlanta on a quest for a better life. As a result of their absence, I became what I refer to as a community baby. My aunts would all take turns taking care of me. This led to my feeling that no matter where I went, I truly did not belong. I began a people pleasing campaign in pursuit of excelling at everything I did so that people would want me around.

My entire life began to change during my freshman year of high school when allegations of sexual abuse threatened to destroy the unstable foundation that I once had. This incident resulted in me moving from one family member's household to another. As a result of the stress and pressure from my family problems, I attempted suicide. Luckily enough I was not successful. One of my uncles decided that it was his turn to join the committee to be my savior for the hour, and I moved to Atlanta. My mother had moved to Houston, Texas for a job opportunity. My uncle was working hard to care for a wife and three children all under the age of five at the time. As a result of financial hardships, we did not have a car or a phone.

I was in a deep depression. I went to school every day, but I did not connect with anyone. However, I made good grades so no one seemed to know or care. My boy friend back home in Alabama became my life line. He had a part time job, so we would schedule times for me to go to the pay phone and call him collect a couple times per week. It was on one of those phone calls that we arranged that I would come home for a visit to attend the prom. We never attended the prom; instead we made a baby, and I continued the generational cycle of teen pregnancy in my family. After becoming aware of my pregnancy, my uncle decided this was more than he could handle and sent me back to live with my grandmother in Alabama. My grandmother agreed that I could live with her until after the baby was born, but put her foot down and said she raised her kids and grandkids; she would not raise her great grand child. Thus the decision was made that at the end of the school year I would go to live with my mother who had moved back to Atlanta.

My transcript depicted the trails of dysfunction and the instability that existed in my life. Wow, now I was living in Atlanta with my mother, a woman I really did not know, with a baby trying to learn how to function within the dysfunction of my world.

My first glimmer of hope came when I entered the local Alternative School. The alternative school had a daycare so that my baby could attend school with me every day. I will never forget that on the first day of school the principal held an assembly and stated that a student could attend my alternative school with zero credits and graduate in two years. The principal was shortly removed from the school because of allegations of misconduct against a student, and an interim principal was brought on board. I was a junior at this time and became very excited that I could possibly graduate a year early. The counselor provided each of us with a schedule and a list of courses needed to graduate. This became what I now understand was my first introduction to goal setting. I mapped out all the courses I needed and the amount of time I needed to spend in each course in order to graduate a year early.

After experiencing some success with my completion plan, I shared my plan with my counselor and she became a dream killer. It became obvious that she did not share the vision of the previous administrator when she told me not to get my hopes up because completing the course work in two years had never been done before. I began to self-sabotage. I began missing school to hang out with my boyfriend who had managed to move to Georgia with a family member to be close to me and the baby. It was my boyfriend that had the insight to establish the foundation for our future. He demanded that I attend school, stating that in order for us to have any type of future together, I must complete high school. I did not miss any more days of school and began to return my focus to my plan.

Research says that the deciding factor in whether or not a student is going to be successful is whether or not they have a caring adult in their lives. The caring adult for me at my alternative school was not the administrators, the counselors, or the teachers. My caring adult was the daycare worker. She was concerned about me whenever I was not at school. She took the time to find out who I was and what was going on in my life. She also took the time to teach me about being a mother and caring for my son when he was sick. She was the reason that I did not give up and drop out. My family loved and cared for me, but if I had dropped out of school, it would not have been a big deal to them. Drop outs were the norm in my family. My supportive adult took a chance on me and sometimes broke the rules to do so. She put me in her car and drove me home when it was pouring down raining. She took the time to get know me and was concerned that I had to walk in rain, sleet or snow down to the train station with a baby bag on one shoulder and a book bag on the other while pushing a stroller. She would keep my son in the daycare even when he had a fever because she knew I had a test or that I was on track to complete a class. I could do no wrong in the eyes of my supportive adult, and I did not want to let her down.

In addition to my dysfunctional family dynamics, the barriers and the obstacles associated with being a teen parent, there were many other obstacles that impeded my educational progress. However, despite instability in school leadership, school counselors not supporting the vision, teachers with low expectations of students success, lack of resources (example, school did not have enough text books for students), I somehow persevered. I would steal the text books over the weekend so I could get ahead in my work. Sadly, there were no social and emotional support programs, but somehow I was able to reach my goal. I completed two years of work in one year and graduated a year early.

Although I graduated, I did so without a post-secondary plan. I attended college but ended up having a second child and found myself still in need of guidance and support from my supportive adult. Every time I would find myself at a crossroad in life, I would drive down the road leading to my alternative school hoping that my supportive adult could offer a word of wisdom that would motivate me to keep trying to find my way. I eventually was able to find my life's purpose which led me to becoming an educator. Once my son graduated from high school, I had an event that honored my supportive adult who had made such a difference in my life and subsequently made a difference in my son's life. Her influence aided in my son graduating from high school and attending college without becoming a teen father, ending the cycle of generational poverty within my family.

My story presents many similarities to students that we work with in our schools each day. How does your school improvement plan meet the needs of these students? How does your parent outreach program meet the needs of the grandparent that does not know how to read or write and does not have transportation to come up to the school? Does your program address the social emotional needs of students who are battling depression, thoughts of suicide, or family dysfunction? How are you addressing the post-secondary needs of your students? Do your students graduate equipped with a post-secondary plan, or is just getting them across the graduation stage your only mission? Does your master schedule reflect a flexible schedule that meets the needs of your students that are working or heads of households, or is it designed to accommodate adult preferences? Is your district allowing your school to be headed by ineffective or unstable leadership? Are low expectations and dysfunctional team dynamics pervasive throughout your school building? If you answered yes to any of the questions above, the next several chapters of this book will provide insight and guidance for effectively transforming your alternative education program or school.

CHAPTER 1

Selecting the Architect

Selecting the correct educational architect or what some refer to as instructional leader for an alternative education program is so very important. The educational architect's role is to develop a vision, select a construction crew, lead the design plan creation, provide direction in the construction of the plan, and guide the implementation of the continuous improvement plan.

Sounds simple doesn't it. Leading an alternative school is a very difficult position. Let's be honest, the leader is being asked in most cases to lead a school of students that were not able to be successful at a traditional school due to their many social /emotional issues. Additionally, he/she must manage a staff of individuals of which many have been a part of the district's dance-of-the-lemons and were moved to the alternative school because they were unsuccessful at a traditional school, causing them to sometimes be bitter and resistant to change. The leader is also deemed to have the responsibility to empower a group of parents and guardians who more than likely did not experience success in school and/or have had such a negative experience with their son or daughter trying to navigate the traditional school maze unsuccessfully that they have completely shut down. In many cases, the students themselves are living on their own as heads of households without any parental support. The leader has to face community perception that considers saving at risk kids not a worthy effort and are not shy about sharing that the school is not welcomed in the community. Sometimes the mission of the educational architect is not even supported by their family, friends and colleagues. Needless to say, leading an alternative school can be a very lonely and isolated position.

Many districts do alternative education schools and programs a disservice by selecting leaders that are ill-equipped. These leaders lack the knowledge, expertise or either the desire to lead the specialized school. The profile of many alternative school leaders fit into one of the three scenarios: the transplant leader, the pension plan leader or the inexperienced leader.

Scenario One: The Transplant Leader

The Transplant Leader that has not been successful in a traditional school setting and the district is not in a position to be able to remove them completely, so they place them in the alternative school with the mindset that he/she will be able to do less damage there. The transplant leader is, in most cases, not equipped with the knowledge and skills needed to successfully meet the needs of the alternative school. If they do have a clue about what is needed, this leader usually has a negative relationship with the district so pushing the initiatives needed to transform the school usually falls on deaf ears. Therefore, ultimate success is not often realized. The leader and the staff begin to become burned out with trying to care for the needs of their students without the necessary resources, so they tend to give up on striving for continuous improvement and pushing for change.

Scenario Two: The Pension Plan Leader

The Pension Plan Leader is the one that is almost ready to retire so we send them to the alternative school just to bide the time needed to get ready to receive their pension. With this type of leader, not much change is going to take place. They are likely going to take the road of least resistance, buying into the motto that this is the way that that it has always been done so keep it the same (Don't rock the boat). More than likely this type of leader is going to make policies and procedures that are more in consideration for the adults than the students. The students that can fit into the one-size- fits-all model that is created are great; our doors are open; the ones that cannot, then sorry, but we cannot save them all.

Scenario Three: The Inexperienced Leader

The Inexperienced Leader has shown some good leadership qualities and is eager to be promoted in the district but has no experience as a principal or working with at-risk students. Knowing that this individual lacks the necessary prerequisite knowledge, we sign them up to try their skills out at the alternative school with the thought that they will do the least amount of damage there. This is the most dangerous type of leader of all. This leader is reading the manual, building the plane and trying to fly it at the same time in the midst of dealing with the never ending crisis of caring for students, staff, family and community issues. Lacking the knowledge of an experienced principal and the skills needed to work with this specialized population, this leader forces the district to embrace the concept of failing forward-- hoping that after experiencing a few years of failure that the inexperienced principal will learn how to transform the school.

These leaders will experience many obstacles and setbacks as they are thrown into the emergency room of education without any training or experience. This leader tends to focus on the wrong work and not what is most important; they lack an understanding of the needs of the school so they hire individuals that lack the knowledge and expertise to drive the work. They tend to make decisions that are divisive in nature and feed into the dysfunctional group dynamics. Many students and staff members will be negatively affected by the leader's inexperience with working with this specialized environment. Ultimately, the school and/or program will not be as successful as it should.

In all the scenarios listed above, the educational leader is placed in an unfair position because their likelihood of success is diminished, not to mention that the staff and students are done a disservice when an ineffective leader is placed at the helm of an alternative school. I urge you to walk into a school and randomly ask students about their administrators. You will quickly develop an understanding of the type of scenario that is being presented in that building based on their responses.

The research outlines that one of the most important factors in the success of any organization is having effective leadership. Just as we take special consideration to staff our blue ribbon schools, we must take that same care to identify effective personnel to work with our most at risk students. When we look at decreasing the dropout rate or increasing graduation rates in the district, the alternative schools have the greatest impact on those numbers. The alternative school is designed to provide a safety net for the student whose needs were not being met at the traditional school. However if the alternative program is not operating at its full potential the district is not going to receive the greatest return on their investment.

A wise friend once told me that what you put into something is what you get out of it. If we continue to put the types of leaders into our alternative schools listed above we will continue to experience limited successful outcomes as a result. This concept of really looking to meet the needs of our most at risk students and schools, building effective leadership to meet the needs of this population has to be the charge of leadership development programs. There are only a few advanced education programs that focus on working with at risk students so district led leadership development programs can play a major role in filling the gap.

One of the leadership development programs in which has been a trailblazer in preparing leaders to work with at risk students is the New Leaders New Schools program. This program recruits potential educational leaders and take them through a paid training program to learn the necessary skills of working at risk students. The potential educational leader is matched to work with a high performing leader for an entire school year in an at risk school to learn how to be an effective leader. Upon the successful completion of both the skills training and the practical on the job training, the leader is deemed eligible to lead a school. It takes this type of intentionality of creating a pipeline of effective leaders to really sustain continuous improvement.

Some district leaders are having a paradigm shift in thinking about the way they are identifying leaders to be at the head of alternative schools. In the section below, an example of this theory of architect selection will be highlighted based on an example from the field.

From Theory to Practice: An Example from the Field:

Associate Superintendent, Mrs. Kelly represented the ideals of district leaders that had a clear understanding that alternative schools and traditional schools are not the same. She had the vision and the tenacity to seek out the funding and resources to support the alternative schools in her district. Through her knowledge and previous experience she had an understanding of the qualities needed to reach the most at-risk student. Drawing on more than 20 years of experience as a teacher and teacher leader, her years working as an assistant principal implementing a transformation initiative, and years of experience leading the transformation of a traditional school to a small school model, she went into a district position equipped for change management. Of her many responsibilities, one was to transform the struggling traditional high schools and alternative schools in the district. She developed a cross functional team to complete a site survey (discussed later in this book) of the alternative schools in the district. Upon review of the reports provided by the cross functional team, a blue print of the three-year scope of work was developed. The district staff was realigned to support the work of transforming the alternative school. A serious search team was formed to review and locate an architect for change to lead the alternative school. Two dynamic assistant principals were appointed based on their track record of successful implementation of transformation initiatives; an additional assistant principal was one who had worked in the school and was promoted to the position. Due to a political decision, a transplant principal was appointed as the lead educational architect. The rule of thought may have been that the three strong assistant principals could over compensate for the transplant principal's ineffectiveness and/ or maybe the transplant would rise to the level of expectation as a result of having such a strong team. This model was a brewing disaster waiting to happen. The assistant principals were constantly doing damage control to fix the mistakes of the principal; the staff was in a state of nervous unrest and the morale was very low. Having insight into the issues brewing at the alternative school, Mrs. Kelly made a decision to remove the transplant leader mid-year and promote one of the assistant principals with the most experience in transformation.

After this decision was made, the true work of transformation began. The school went from being considered a dropout factory to being considered a model alternative school for the state and the nation and receiving accommodations from the United States Department of Education.

The success of an educational institution rises and falls based on effective leadership. In order for us to truly impact the students that have the greatest needs, we must transform our mindset and develop a new model of only selecting the most experienced and most qualified individuals as educational architects in our alternative schools.

CHAPTER 2

The Construction Crew

When thinking about the work of transforming alternative education, it bring to mind HGTV design shows where they demonstrate the renovations of old houses and buildings. One of the transformations that I was able to serve in viewed the transformation as such, and it was labeled the Extreme Makeover Project. It is very interesting to watch the interior design programs showing designers/architects and construction crews working together from the beginning of a project. The designer/architect shares the vision with the crew, and they work out how the scheme will be accomplished. Everyone understands the design objectives, and knows how their tasks contribute. At the end of the program, the show usually depicts the finished project with the client, designer/architect and crew pleased with the outcome.

Making sure that the right people are on board to lead the work is going to propel the transformation initiative forward. Not having the right people on board will stifle the project and distract the team from focusing on the right work. It is also very important to develop a collaborative team approach when selecting your construction crew members. Select a team of individuals that will work closely with the candidate. Establish a criteria or idea of the qualifications, characteristics, and experience level of the type of candidate that will be the best fit for your team. Develop an instrument to tally the points based on the candidate's qualifications, characteristics and experience level to determine which candidate should be added to the construction crew. Below are two examples or scenarios of ineffective selection of construction crew members:

Scenario One: Internal Promotion

Ms. Clark is currently an English teacher in your school and has applied to be an English instructional coach. She is a very good teacher and works well with the other members in her department. She refuses, however, to attend the mandatory professional learning sessions on Saturdays, states that she is not able to attend conferences and workshops due to family obligations and refuses to take on any additional responsibilities that she is not paid to do. Mr. Black is also a good English teacher that has applied for the same position. He is very passionate about the work and has a vision for how the English department needs to change but is very aggressive in his approach, so the team is sometimes offended by him. He does, however, attend all the mandatory professional learning opportunities on Saturdays and seeks out additional workshops and conferences to improve his craft. After interviewing all the internal and external candidates, the team finds that none of the candidates have a track record of increasing student achievement. The team is given a district directive that an instructional coach must be hired as soon as possible in order to be in compliance with the school improvement implementation timeline. The team selects Ms. Clark as the instructional coach in hopes that she can use her relationship building skills to move the English department to reach the goals. The English department shuts down and complies only on the surface under the leadership of the instructional coach. The team holds private meetings complaining about how the new instructional coach was able to be promoted and discuses the fact that she was not actively involved in the implementation of the school improvement initiatives prior to being promoted. Hiring this member to the construction crew caused a major setback to implementing the transformation project in the area of English. The first year was spent struggling to overcome internal resistance and developing team building strategies to combat the dysfunctional team dynamics rather than focusing on strategies to increase student achievement.

Scenario Two: Hiring You Who You Know

A graduation coach position is opened at your school. This is a highly sought after position since the district has implemented a very aggressive plan to increase the graduation rate. To attract top talent to the position, the district has increased the salary for the position without increasing the qualifications required of the graduation coach. Numerous candidates apply for the position, and the team is flooded with referrals and recommendations for candidates. Two internal candidates apply. One candidate has over twenty years of experience working as a registrar at the school and has furthered her education to obtain a masters and specialist degree and a certification in school counseling. The other internal candidate is an exemplary teacher in the building with over ten years of experience and has furthered her education to receive a master's degree in school counseling. After interviewing over twenty candidates the team decides on an external candidate that has a degree and certification in school counseling and experience working in alternative education. The principal decides after the selection meeting that she is not satisfied with any of the candidates interviewed. Instead the principal decides that she wants to hire a candidate that she has worked with in a previous district. The candidate is a teacher that does not have any experience or education related to counseling or student support services. The principal is convinced that she is the best person for the job and believes her work ethic will over compensate for the lack of knowledge and experience. As a result of the new hire, the student support team becomes dysfunctional and a hostile work environment is created. The team voiced their belief that favoritism and nepotism was occurring. Members of the team began to work in isolation to avoid arguments and sometimes volatile meetings occurred; experienced and knowledgeable staff requested transfers to remove themselves from the unhealthy work environment. The goals and milestones of this department are over shadowed by personnel conflicts.

In both scenarios above, the selected candidates possessed positive characteristics that could add value to any team. Given the underlying situations, however, the positives did not outweigh the negative impact of hiring.

Inheriting a Dysfunctional Team

Sometimes an architect can inherit a dysfunctional construction crew. Below are examples of a dysfunctional construction crews:

Scenario One: A Line in the Sand

The principal at the beginning of the school year presented the state of the school and the strategic vision to the leadership team. An organizational chart is created and distributed to outline the duties and responsibilities of each member of the team. The construction team members include a school improvement administrator, assistant principal over testing and curriculum, assistant principal over discipline and student support services, assistant principal over operations, a graduation coach, counselors, social workers and math and English instructional coaches. The school improvement administrator, eager to move the strategic vision of the principal, begins to share examples of past test preparation plans with the instructional coaches.

The curriculum assistant principal becomes livid. She is infuriated that the school improvement administrator has shared anything with her instructional coaches without discussing it with the assistant principal first. Believing that the school improvement specialist was trying to show her up or make her look bad, the curriculum assistant principal began a campaign to rally the other assistant principals to join the cause stating the school improvement specialist is not a team player and works in isolation to receive all the accolades and credit. As a result of the dysfunction, the instructional coaches feel like they are in the middle of two divorced parents and become stagnant in their ability to carry out their jobs effectively.

Scenario Two: Broken Promises

An important part of any leader's strategic vision is to develop the capacity of staff and to develop a succession plan to replace staff member when they retire or move to different schools or positions. Ms. Green had not only developed a mental succession plan, but she shared it with the affected individuals so that they could prepare themselves accordingly. The head counselor was only two years away from retirement, so the associate counselor was made aware that she would be moving to the head counselor position. In preparation for her new role, the associate counselor went back to school to work on her educational specialist degree. The counseling clerk was in school to obtain a certification in school counseling in preparation to be promoted to the associate counselor position. The moment of truth came and the head counselor announced her retirement. However, the principal began to have second thoughts about her succession plan and scheduled interviews for external candidates. She decided to hire an external candidate that came highly recommended from a colleague whose professional opinion she truly valued. She not only hired the candidate as a counselor to replace the retired counselor, but she made her the head counselor-- discounting promises made to the current employees. This decision led to an overall feeling of distrust among the staff. In fighting began to occur leading to a visible divide noticeable internal and external of the organization. The principal Ms. Green decided to go ahead and retire and leave the drama for the next lucky administrator to handle.

In both scenarios the team members are so focused on their own personnel issues they become emotionally drained causing them to be unable to address the students' issues at the appropriate level. Let's be honest. In a hospital if the doctors and nurses are all fighting, how are they able to care for the wounds of the patients coming in for help? We have a lot of emotionally unhealthy students entering the doors of the alternative schools only to encounter unhealthy adults assigned as their care givers. How do we ensure that we have the right individuals on board and that those individuals are focused on the right work?

Extreme Times Call for Extreme Measures

Alternative education programs are structures that support students that are most at risk for dropping out of high school. I would consider them to be the intensive care unit of the educational system. Like the medical ICU unit that employs specialized doctors and nurses, we must employ staff that is highly specialized and trained to work in alternative education programs. Imagine putting a pediatrician and pediatric nursing staff in charge of running a trauma center that receives multiple gunshot wounds a day. Imagine the number of casualties or deaths that would occur daily due to the lack of experience, passion, and expertise needed to effectively care for the unique population. We would think that this was medical malpractice. However, we commit educational malpractice everyday by placing educational leaders, teachers and support staff in alternative education settings who lack the experience, passion and expertise needed to effect change with this unique population of students. The number of casualties is alarming as we look at the dropout rates which provide a glimpse into the death toll of all the hopes, dreams and unrealized potential of the students impacted by our decisions. Let us be radical about selecting and preparing our crew members to effectively work with our at promise students. Factors to consider when selecting Crew Members include: Emotional Intelligence, Diversity, and Innovative. Daniel Goldman's book on Emotional Intelligence provides a list of identified skills that I believe are the cornerstone of the makings of a great construction crew. Below is a short description of these skills:

Self Awareness

Self awareness is the ability of individuals to recognize their own and other people's emotions; to discriminate between different feelings and label them appropriately, and to use emotional information to guide thinking and behavior. Understanding what thoughts sparks off certain feelings and what feelings are behind certain actions is an important skill for alternative educators to possess.

Managing Emotions

It is important to realize what is behind feelings. Beliefs have a fundamental effect on the ability to act and on how things are done. Many people continually give themselves negative messages. Hope can be a useful asset. Finding ways to deal with anger, fear, anxiety and sadness in the classroom is essential. Understanding how to manage situations when emotions get the upper hand in order to gain time to judge what is being said or done in the appropriate manner is imperative.

Empathy

Empathy is related to the level of an individual's ability to evaluate situations and act appropriately. To take others perspective, listen without being carried away by personal emotions. It is important to be able to distinguish between the action and the reaction "What students say or do and the educator's personal reactions and judgements."

Communication

The ability to develop quality relationships has a positive effect on the teacher and the student. What feelings are being communicated from your staff? Enthusiasm and optimism are contagious as are pessimism and negativity. Being able to express thoughts and ideas without negative feelings of anger or passivity is a key asset.

Co-operation

Having the insight of knowing how and when to take the lead and how to follow is essential for effective cooperation. The art of working together for a common goal is essential. It is important to recognize the value and contributions in others and encourage participation rather than complaining and worrying about who will get the credit. An effective team member should participate in shared decision making, take responsibility for tasks, and follow through on commitments.

Food for thought

How does your team currently make hiring decisions? It is very difficult from a cover letter and resume to glean whether or not the individual possesses the key emotional intelligence skills, whether the individual really has a passion, desire or understanding of how to work with students of poverty and/or of diverse backgrounds. What do you do when the ideal candidate is not in you applicant pool? Have you developed internal onboarding professional development programs to train new staff on the essential skills necessary to effectively work with your unique population? Do you have a process to remove ineffective staff members that after training and support still are not performing at the appropriate level?

Alternative schools and programs are the Intensive Care Units of the education system. If we don't do our due diligence in effectively selecting, preparing and managing staff to work with at promise students our death rates, which are our drop-out rates, will continue to increase. Can you look at every student on your drop-out list and say to the family "we did everything we could to save your child?" If not, why not?

CHAPTER 3

The Site Survey

To lay a solid foundation for any transformation initiative the first step is completing a comprehensive site survey also sometimes referred to as a root cause analysis. A **site survey** is an evaluation or assessment of an area where work is proposed. The site survey is designed to gather the necessary information so that a continuous improvement design plan or blueprint can be created. The site survey is a comprehensive look at the achievement data, demographic data, the community resources, the strengths and weakness of the human capital and any additional data points deemed necessary to guide the scope of work. The site survey aids in determining the obstacles to successful implementation of a transformation initiative and identifies areas of opportunity.

There is not a one-size-fits-all approach to transforming an alternative school. Each school has its own DNA structure. One must understand that systematic change will not occur overnight just as the issues present in the school or program did not occur overnight. Another school of thought is we cannot change a problem with the same mind that created the problem, so it may be helpful to bring in someone outside the school or program to assist in the review of the data. We sometimes feel the need to make excuses and discount the data because we take it personally when the data reveals undesired results.

Failure to take the time that is necessary to complete the site survey effectively is one of the greatest pitfalls in the implementation of transformation. A contractor would not start building a house without a site survey or a blueprint, and an educational architect should not begin making decisions regarding restructuring a school without doing the same.

Things to remember when completing a successful site survey:

1. Step 1: Determine what happened. Remember it is whatever the data says it is. Don't read between the lines. Just record the data in a graphic organizer or some sort of visual aid. It is very important to identify the data sources for each data point recorded.

2. Step 2: Determine how long the data point has existed by doing a data trend analysis. What is the likelihood that data trends will remain constant or change?

3. Step 3: Determine how pervasive the problem is. Is the problem limited to the individual student level, the teacher level or organizational level?

4. Step 4: Look for the good. Never take the stance that everything is wrong. Even in the worst of organizations, good things are happening.

5. Step 5: Share the data with the team. Collaboratively determine what the focus of the blueprint or strategic plan should be.

Example: One Alternative is considered one of the lowest performing schools in the district due to their graduation rate and math standardized test scores. After ten years of having the same principal, the school experienced a year of inconsistent leadership. The mindset was that everything was wrong; in reality, there were a lot of positive things going on in the school. However, the instructional leader came in with distrust for key staff members and began to dismantle key structures which led to throwing the school into a state of nervous unrest. The result was that data flat lined that year and no progress was made.

It is important to be transparent with staff about concerns and get them involved in the root cause analysis. Focus on the process and not the person.

Example:

We have had three years of declining test scores. Why? What have we tried in the past? What does the research say about best practices to improve test scores? What do you think that we should try? How will we monitor and track our progress?

This laser-focused approach will assist in developing a continuous process for school improvement.

CHAPTER 4

The Blue Print

The blue print or the school strategic plan is one of the most valuable documents that a school design team can create. Most teams create this document as act of compliance. If used effectively it can be the road map to transforming a school. The blue print needs to address all issues identified by the site survey. Understanding that all the issues that are identified will not be to be able to be addressed in one school year the team must prioritize the needs and determine which initiatives will have the greatest impact. This is not an easy task, and everyone on the design team may not agree on the pressing priorities. It may be beneficial to employ the assistance of an external individual or organization to assist the team in mapping out their three to five year plan.

Things to remember when designing the blueprint:

1. Just because an initiative worked at another school does not mean that it will work for your school. Remember every school has it on DNA.

2. Check the cultural competence of your design team. They may be developing plans to address the needs of a population other than the population that you serve. Example (How does your family engagement plan address homeless families?)

3. Focus on doing a few things well instead of trying to do a lot of things mediocre.

Scenario One:

The principal and assistant principal have competing priorities. The principal has gone to a conference and has decided to adopt a new literacy strategy that he feels is the perfect solution to increase the reading level of students school wide. The assistant principal has worked with literacy across the curriculum for several years with a similar demographic and has seen positive results in using a different approach. The staff, witnessing a divide in the leadership, feels torn and fails to fully invest in the literacy initiative.

Scenario Two:

The State Department of Education has deemed the school to be one of the lowest performing in the state. If rapid improvement is not made this school year, chances are the school will be closed or taken over by the state. The leadership, feeling the pressure from the state and district, began to move quickly, mandating and implementing many new initiatives. By December, the staff was completely burned out and acting out of compliance instead of truly implementing the initiative with fidelity.

CHAPTER 5

The Big Picture

As educators, we are sometimes very reactive. Constantly putting out fires and handling the day to day battles of running a school. Very few truly look at the big picture. What is the vision of your school or program? What should your students be able to do once they complete their course of study? What role does the school play in the community in which it serves? When transforming a school, these are questions that should be asked and answered. The school cannot answer these questions in a vacuum. This is a dialogue that should take place with the community at large.

Examples of questions that should be pondered:

1. What are the resources in the community?

2. What is the employment outlook and the related needs of the community?

3. What are the soft-skills needed by students to obtain employment?

4. What are the needs of the school that the community could address?

5. What are the post-secondary options for students?

Scenario One: Drop Out Crisis

Pittman High School was experiencing an increase in their dropout rate. The students were turning sixteen and going to work in the factories in the local community. The leadership of the school reached out to local chamber of commerce to discuss this issue of dropout and the community launched a pledge to graduate campaign. New rules were established that in order to obtain a job in the local factories an individual would have to demonstrate current enrollment in school or a high school diploma.

Scenario Two: Community School

Washington High School was a school with many unique needs. A high rate of teen pregnancy, students with low self-efficacy, homelessness, limited access to health care, issues with trauma and mental illness were just some of the serious concerns. The school held a community forum to discuss the issues within the school and community. The school became a hub to create a circle of support for the students and their families. Medical, Dental and Vision vans were scheduled to come to the school on a consistent basis. As a result, the school began to offer affordable health care informational sessions on a quarterly basis and began offering job skills training sessions for students. Mental health agencies provided services and facilitated training sessions on parenting, anger management, and conflict resolution. The faith based community provided mentors and service learning experiences. It is amazing the difference we can make when the school and community combine resources.

CHAPTER 6

Zoning

The term zoning is defined as the practice of designing mapped zones to regulate the design and compatibility of development. In most alternative education schools and programs, students are placed or referred that the other schools deem unworthy of development in their home school. What is your practice or procedure for enrolling new students? Is there a transition team from the home school and the alternative school that meets to discuss the strengths, weaknesses and needs of the student? Are any diagnostic screenings done to assess students' needs?

The process for enrolling new students is so very important. This is a time to find out the academic and social emotional needs of a student. Through the use of a psycho-social history, important information can be obtained to see if mental health services are needed for the student and their families. The facilitation of a reading and math diagnostic assessment can assist the counselor and teacher in proper course placement, and academic support programs should be available to students from day one. The alternative education student population presents many unique needs. Identifying those needs early can allow the team to develop an individual success plan for the student to increase the likelihood that the student will be successful. When developing the zoning plans and policies a great place to start is a review of the National Alternative Education Exemplary Practice Standards. Below is an excerpt from the document.

EXEMPLARY PRACTICE 7.0: TRANSITION PLANNING AND SUPPORT

- Clear transition criteria and procedures are in place to address student enrollment, transfers, and reintegration, if applicable, to a traditional setting at exemplary nontraditional or alternative schools.

- Transition plans include college and career readiness support for high school students.

- School counselors or transition specialists are specifically trained to address student transitions.

- The transition process ensures the nontraditional or alternative school is the most appropriate placement based on the student's effective and affective needs, academic requirements, and post-baccalaureate goals.

Indicators of Quality Programming:

7.1 A screening committee to ensure the placement is most appropriate for the student's specific effective and affective needs, academic requirements, and post-baccalaureate goals is in place at exemplary nontraditional or alternative schools.

7.2 A formal transition process for students from entry to exit which includes the following elements: an orientation which consists of rapport building, assessment of the student, IEP review, information and record sharing regarding the student, short and long-term goal setting, development of an individualized student plan, and other mechanisms designed to orient the student to the alternative education setting is in place at exemplary schools.

7.3 Transition planning and the student plan afford students the opportunity to maintain and accelerate their current progress toward matriculation or graduation.

7.4 A Student Support Team (SST) is established that consists of educators from the school of origin, educators from the nontraditional or alternative school, the student, parents/guardians and other trained transitional personnel. The team is directly involved in all aspects of the transition process including assessment, planning, and implementation of the student's transition plan.

7.5 Transition planning includes referral and timely access to community agencies, and support services such as: mental health, public health, family support, housing, physical fitness activities, and other youth services.

7.6 When appropriate, students are provided with opportunities to develop and maintain supportive links to the school of origin.

7.7 Student areas of strength and growth are addressed as part of transition in, throughout, and upon exit of the nontraditional or alternative school.

7.8 Prior to a student's entrance and exit from the school, transition services are coordinated by the SST with all appropriate entities to ensure successful entry into the student's next educational setting or workforce.

7.9 Within the bounds of the Family Educational Rights and Privacy Act (FERPA), information sharing (availability of pertinent records) takes place between the school of origin, the nontraditional or alternative school, and other social service organizations. Copies of the student cumulative academic file should be sent to the nontraditional or alternative school to ensure adherence to second language, special needs, or medical plans, to establish accurate student schedules, and to ensure the student's areas of academic strength and growth are known and used by the nontraditional or alternative school

CHAPTER 7

Demolition

"Comforting the discomforted and

upsetting the comfortable"

One of the big questions that must be asked is: Are our policies and procedures established to meet the needs of the students that we serve, or are they built for adult preferences. Does our bell schedule maximize instruction in a way that is designed to support student needs or does it seek to satisfy adults? Do our school day schedule and attendance plans accommodate our stakeholders' needs? Are we truly an alternative school, or are we a traditional school in drag? What are the benefits of attending the alternative school versus the traditional school? Are we a drop-out factory? Are we the school that students go to drop out?

Having this type of conversation can spark a bit of emotion and make some faculty and staff members uncomfortable. If a policy or practice is creating a barrier to student success, it should be reviewed and then changed or abolished. If a student was not successful in a traditional school environment and the alternative school employs the same policies and procedures, then the student is not going to be successful at the alternative school.

Example:

All for One High School was having a major problem with attendance. A policy was put into place that if a student missed three days of school, the student would be withdrawn. A review of this policy revealed that this created a revolving door of entry and withdrawals finally resulting in an increase in the number of students dropping out. The design team came up with a plan to address this concern by allowing the student to set their own schedule much like a college campus. Students scheduled classes when it was convenient for them. If students worked the night shift and would have difficultly arriving to school at 8:00 a.m., they could schedule their first class to begin at 3rd period and would not have to arrive at school until 10:30 a.m. Why penalize students for their life situations?

Personalized learning is a term that is very popular these days in the educational setting. How do we personalize the learning experiences for our students? We must begin with conversations with our students. Student voice is so very important. The students are our customers. Our job is to fulfill the educational needs of our customers. We sometimes take an all or nothing approach. We establish total virtual learning centers or we are afraid to use technology at all. Why not develop an educational delivery model wherein students could engage in a virtual course (totally online), a direct instruction model, and a blended learning course (Mixture of online with direct core teacher support). Give students the option to select the model of learning that best fits their needs and learning styles.

CHAPTER 8

Framing

"Mission, Vision, and Core Values"

What is the vision and mission of your school? Studies show that at least fifty percent of staff and students do not know the mission and vision of their school. The mission and vision set the tone for what strategies are implemented as well as why they are implemented, and it explains the belief systems of the organization for all stakeholders. Every decision that is made within the school needs to be measured against the mission, the vision and core values of the school. How often are the mission and vision reviewed? What input was given from the stakeholders in the development of that vision and mission? Has a framework for onboarding new staff been developed with the mission and vision in mind?

The mission and vision set the framework for culture of the school. It establishes the school's way of doing things, the focus of the work and the expectations for all involved.

What does this really mean? It means that the staff must develop a common language and belief system about the goals and the direction of work of the school. If the mission is to be accomplished, then what will be the actions of the staff and the students? What will be the roles of the stake-holders? How will the success or lack of success toward accomplishing the mission and vision be measured? This is the foundation for which all work will be measured. Ask yourself, are we measuring up to our vision and mission? If so, what's next? If not, why not?

CHAPTER 9

Interior Design
and Exterior Finish

When students enter the doors of an alternative school they are in search of something different. The traditional school structure and programs did not prove to be a place where the student, for whatever reason, could be successful. What custom features does your school offer catered to the unique needs of the population you serve? In a previous chapter, we discussed demolishing old and out of date structures that are not meeting the needs of students. This chapter will discuss strategies for designing programs that create a circle of support that fosters student success.

Let's face it; students come to us with many social and emotional needs. However, most schools are only equipped to focus on the academic needs of students. So what do you do when a student is a teen parent head of household because both of her parents are addicted to drugs and she is also caring for her younger sister as well? We all know that Maslow's hierarchy of needs states that it is hard to focus on self-actualization and goal attainment when your basic needs are a concern. There are thousands of horror stories of what our students are faced with as they walk the halls of our school daily.

The sad thing is you cannot see their struggle by their appearance. However, their behavior may provide a clue to their internal crisis. Often, we focus on the symptoms of tardiness, absence, lack of homework completion, and academic failure without a thought of the root cause and external factors that are impacting students' academic engagement and performance. Although I have no scientific evidence, I truly believe that extreme poverty may cause post -traumatic stress syndrome and other mental health challenges. Many schools are faced with students that struggle with a sense of hopelessness, depression and anxiety; many of those same students, as well as others, are using substances such as marijuana and prescription drugs to self-medicate and cope with life's challenges.

ASCD Research on the "whole child" approach to educating students suggests that schools should ensure that students are Healthy, Safe, Engaged, Supported and Challenged. How does your school address these areas? Below are some examples of how these tents of the whole child can be accomplished through programs designed to empower, motivate and encourage students to be successful.

Health & Wellness

In African American and other minority communities, access to proper health care is often a challenge and addressing mental illness can sometimes be viewed as taboo. Creating partnership with the local health department, hospitals, doctors' offices, dentist, eye doctors and mental health facilities will be key to addressing these needs. Traditionally, we identify that students have health related needs and we refer the family to community agencies. A large percentage of these referrals go unanswered because of the family's lack of transportation or the need for parents to take off work to accompany the students to the appointment. Building a community school model where these services are provided in the school setting remove the barriers of accesses.

Safe

When we think of school safety usually the first things that come to mind are crime, guns, drugs, bullying. It is important that the school but safe guards against these issues. However it is also very important that we safe guards students psychological health as well.

Does your staff take special care to interact with student demonstrating dignity and respect building their sense of self-worth and self-esteem? Does your culture promote that mistakes are a part of the learning process? Students don't always arrive at school understanding how to fit into the culture of the school. Special care should be taken to inform students and families that they are welcomed in the school and focus is to address all their needs to make school a safe place for individual and collective successful outcomes.

Engaged

Students should have the option to be engaged in school or program that will meet their needs. Understanding that every students needs are different our schools' program offerings should not be a one size fits all or cookie cutter. Be Creative. Create flexible scheduling options for students. Think of the college model where students come to school at times that best fits their life schedule. Students are given a list of courses needed to graduate and a list of course offerings and design schedules that meet the needs of their unique challenges.

The master schedule should provide various options to include day and evening courses, direct instruction, blended learning and virtual options for students. A continuum of services.

Implementing co-curricular programs can be used as a way to increase student engagement. Most alternative education programs don't offer sports and fine arts options. Adding intramural sports and clubs can make major impact on student engagement.

Student voice is so important. Have a student to service on the leadership team or develop a student principals advisory to provide insight into operational decision making.

Challenged

The nature of working in an alternative education setting is that student normally enter the building presenting major learning gaps in basic foundational knowledge in reading and math. The challenge becomes how do you remediate the learning gaps and accelerate the students to fulfill graduation requirements and achieve on high stakes tests. We must remove the myth that alternative students cannot achieve at high levels.

We have to become specialist in diagnosing the issues and prescribing the correct instructional strategies to ensure academic success.

CHAPTER 10

Progress Monitoring

A wise person once said: "Tell your own story, or someone else will." In this day and age people want to know "what's your data story?" One of the most important tasks is learning what projects are worth measuring and monitoring. A good rule of thumb is: if you are going to put in the time to implement monitoring, then a data analysis component should be included as well. In alternative education, our data sometimes tells a different story than a traditional school setting, so a lot of educators tend to shy away from the use of data or dismiss it as not being an accurate reflection of the work. Rather than shying away from it, use the data to create a new narrative for your school or program. Have sessions to explain to stakeholders exactly what the data says and what it means in relation to the school's mission.

Example:

Model Alternative was highlighted in the local newspaper for having a nine percent graduation rate although they graduated 120 students that school year. The matrix used for calculating graduation rate in the state measure not how many students graduated but how many students graduated within four years after beginning 9th grade. Model alternative school reviewed their data to recognize that they were receiving students that were past their cohort graduation year, and would always be considered dropouts. They changed the narrative. The school began highlighting their completion rate the percentage of students that entered the school that graduated. The school began a marketing campaign to highlight qualitative data on the obstacles overcome by their students with successful outcomes to demonstrate the collective impact of their school and community partnerships. Model Alternative changed the narrative, and the perception of the school changed from a drop out factory to a school making a difference in the community.

In order to change the narrative, listed below are some guiding questions related to data that all alternative schools should ask.

Demographic Data:

Who are our students (teen parents? the Homeless? heads of households)?

What trends do we see in our population (gender, age, and ethnicity)?

What are the community factors that may influence school performance (employment rate, housing, crime rates)?

Enrollment:

Where do they come from (school of origin, community, judicial system, department of family and children's services)?

What factors affected attendance at home school (medical, legal, behavior)?

What does the student transcript reveal (testing history, course history, progress toward graduation)?

Student Learning Data

What evidence can we collect that demonstrates that our students are learning/achieving (student mastery checklist, performance on formative and summative assessments, course completion)?

What do we know about each individual student and how they learn (diagnostic math and reading assessments, learning styles inventory, digital learning survey)?

School Process Data:

How does our entrance or enrollment process impact student success (The number of students that enroll v. number of students that complete)?

How does our attendance plan impact student success (The number of days a student missed at traditional school versus number of days missed at the alternative school)?

How will our master schedule/ bell schedule impact student success (The number of courses student are able to complete at a traditional school versus alternative school, Are academic supports built into the school day)?

How does our discipline policy impact student learning? (How has the student's behavior changed as a result of being enrolled in the alternative versus the traditional school)?

Perception Data:

What is the faculty and staff saying about the school?

What are the students' perceptions of the school?

What are the parents and other stakeholders perceiving about the school?

A school's operational processes must be designed with intention to ensure continuous improvement and successful outcomes for students. Some examples of some operational progresses are:

Implementation of common planning time: Sometimes in alternative education settings, it is difficult to obtain buy-in of teachers to fully engage in professional learning communities because most alternative settings are full of singletons (One teacher teaching each course). However, this is a key structural area for school improvement. Common planning time should include collaborative planning sessions where teacher teams focus on implementing effective instructional strategies that are both rigorous and relevant for students. It is important to use data protocols to evaluate student work and to monitor student progress.

After each grading period, it is important to implement a data presentation process where teachers present and defend their data. They discuss course failure rates, not in terms of numbers, but in terms of what students know and do not know based on mastery of standards. Additionally, support staff support and present data based on other key data points. For example, the counselor presents student graduation or course completion rates; the social worker presents on attendance rates; the parent liaison presents on parent engagement numbers. Collectively this is referred to as a quarterly State of the School presentation.

Another great process is the implementation of a treatment team. This team meets bi-monthly and takes a comprehensive approach to reviewing data drilled down to the student level. The team consists of multiple team members, and data is presented on students' academic progress, attendance, behavior, graduation status and social/emotional needs.

Bimonthly leadership team meetings are also important so that the distributive leadership model is engrained in the school culture. This time is used to review leading indicators that affect school improvement. This should not be used as an operations meeting.

A Model for School Improvement

There are many school improvement intervention models. I have taken multiple models based on action research and designed what I refer to as the Five Phase Model to Ensure Student Success. Like the doctor who practices medicine, and the lawyer who practices law, teachers practice education. Just as a doctor who prescribes a medicine and the patient does not show improvement changes his prescription or treatment, a teacher should not continue to implement instructional strategies that are not meeting the needs of students.

DAS Five Phase Model to Ensure Student Success

Phase I. Diagnosis

(Using Data to Drive Instruction)

- Use data usage and analysis to determine needs
- Identify and prioritize needs
- Design and develop a data gathering system
- Data Collection and Displaying Data

Phase II. Treatment Planning

(Curriculum Mapping)

- Development of plans, goals and objectives
- Alignment of Instructional Program
- Dual/Double Lesson Planning

Phase III. Prescription Delivery

(Standards Based Instruction)

- Engaging Pedagogy
- Instructional practices and strategies
- Differentiated Instruction
- Inquiry Based Instruction

Phase IV. MRI Assessment

(Common Assessments)

- Curriculum-Based Assessment Strategies
- Progress Monitoring
- Response to Intervention

Phase V. Collaboration and/or Referral

(Treatment Teams)

- Peer Coaching and Mentoring

- Analyzing Student Work

- Case Conferencing

DAS Five Phase Model to Ensure Student Success

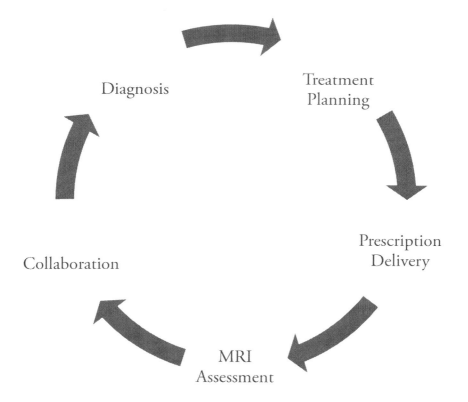

CHAPTER 11

Open House

I like to say that alternative education schools are the best kept secret in education. The success outcomes that we receive from students that are considered the most at risk for dropping out is amazing work. Just like a model home presents its unique features, it is important that we highlight the unique features of our schools and programs. Listed and briefly outlined below are the top twenty promising practices that have proven to have an impact on student achievement in alternative education settings.

Promising Practices:

1. Believe Orientations- Required as a part of the enrollment process. Students are introduced to the school and a new way of thinking. Students bury past mistakes and failures and plant seeds to start their future.

2. Begin with the End in Mind- Required as a part of enrollment, students meet with their counselor to review courses needed to graduate, develop a graduation plan, set their graduation date and sign a pledge to graduate.

3. Lunch & Learn- Weekly programs are designed to address post-secondary options available to students.

4. Advisory- Two days per week a block is scheduled for a focus on building relationships and meeting the social and emotional needs of the students.

5. Increased Learning Time- Three days per week, a block is scheduled to address the academic supports needed based on universal screeners and teacher recommendation.

6. Student Led Conferences- Quarterly, students must present their goals, progress, next steps to their advisor, parent or advocate prior to enrollment for next courses.

7. Flexible Opportunities for Student Learning- Flex Scheduling- Students are able to determine the pace at which they will engage in completing graduation requirement by taking advantage of day and evening courses, Saturday school and summer courses.

8. Full Service Childcare Center- A childcare center is housed on campus open for teen parents during school hours.

9. Student Voice- Principal's Advisory meet monthly where students provide insight on what changes are needed in the school.

10. School Based Medical and Dental Services- Bi-weekly school-based clinic free of charge for students.

11. Mental Health Services- School based individual/ family counseling, anger management classes, smoking cessation classes are provided on campus for students.

12. Student Clubs & Organizations- Student clubs are an excellent way to build relationship and a sense of connection to the school. Some clubs include: Success Ambassadors, Leading Ladies, Leading Men, Teen Parent Circle of Support, Book/ Writers clubs, Drama Clubs, Students Against Destructive Decisions Club, Technology club.

13. Mentoring- School Site Based Mentoring Program- Students meet with Mentor weekly during Lunch.

14. Intra-mural and Extra-Mural sports programs- Students that engage in sports programs reduce drop out risk, build relationships and connection to school.

15. Career and Technical Education- CTE programs add the relevance for academics and post-secondary options for students.

16. Work-Based Learning- Work based learning addresses an immediate need of providing financial support, teaches soft skills and assist in graduation completion through credit attainment.

17. College & Career Fieldtrips- Too see is to know. Students are given monthly exposure to post–secondary options through engaging in college tours & career-related field trips.

18. 9th grade Academy- A specialized program for over aged 8th graders. Students that have experience failure in elementary and middle school are given the option of accelerating their graduation timeline and graduate within 2 to 3 years instead of the 4 year traditional track.

19. Dual Enrollment- Students are given the option to enroll in a technical college, 2 or 4 year university while being enrolled in high school.

20. Student and Staff Acknowledgment- It is so very important that student and staff are acknowledged often when promoting efforts to implement continuous improvement. Examples: Dream Builders of the Month (Teachers) Dream Team Builders of the month (Support staff); Quarterly 212 degree awards; We Love Our Teachers Day (Valentines); Staff All- Star Awards Ceremony; (Selected by staff members

based on schools core values); A & B honor roll lunches and awards day, Lunch with principal for top scores on high stakes testing, doing school parties, PBIS incentives.

ABOUT THE AUTHOR

Dr. Lateshia Woodley, LCC NCC
Dynamic Achievement Solutions

Dr. Lateshia Woodley is a Counseling Psychologist and Educational Consultant that specializes in transformation initiatives and change management. For the past several years, Dr. Woodley has worked with academic, community and private sectors bringing about positive change.

Dr. Woodley has a proven track record of designing programs and interventions that increase productivity and performance. She has worked with special projects which include: Middle School to High School Transformation, New Teacher Mentoring Programs, District Wide Advisory Programs, School Based Mentoring Programs, School Improvement and High Stakes Testing Intervention Programs, College Readiness Initiatives, School Improvement Grant Program, Georgia Department of Education Alternative Education Transition Committee, and the National Alternative Education Planning Committee.

Dr. Woodley has worked with organizations such as the Bill and Melinda Gates Foundation's Youth Truth Project and Small School Transformation Initiatives. She served as the counseling director for the Morehouse College

Upward Bound Program. She facilitated courses with the Youth Entrepreneurs of Atlanta. She facilitated workshops and trainings with the Institute of Student Achievement. She has been a presenter at several educational conferences most notably the Model Schools Conference. She has worked with the Georgia Department of Education evaluating the 21st Century Program, Supplemental Educational Services, and Homeless Education Program.

She is the author of two books titled "Why Did You Choose to Get Pregnant" which is a workbook to guide teen parents through this major life transition and "Issues of the Heart" a reflection journal. She believes that it is important that we provide the stimulus to our environment that will bring about positive change. Her life principle is to be a catalyst that ignites, motivates, and encourages individuals and organizations to reach their full potential.

Made in the USA
Middletown, DE
15 April 2018